Good Girls Don't Cry

This book is dedicated to
my Mother Margaret
and
my sisters
Moira
Ella
and
Janette

Good Girls Don't Cry

Margaret Fulton Cook

Chapman Publishing
1996

Published by
Chapman
4 Broughton Place
Edinburgh EH1 3RX
Scotland

A catalogue record for this volume is
available from the British Library.
ISBN 0-906772-75-3

Chapman New Writing Series
Editor Joy Hendry
ISSN 0953-5306

The publisher acknowledges the financial assistance
of the Scottish Arts Council.

Some of the poems and versions of the poems have
appeared in the following magazines and anthologies:

*Bête Noire, Common Sense, The Echo Room, Gown, New Voices New
Writing (Scottish Child Literary Supplement), Northlight, Out From
Beneath the Boot Issue 3, Paisley Yarns, Poetry & Audience, Poetry
Wales, The Rialto, Scotia Bar 1st of May Poetry Prize anthology,
Scottish Child, Scratch, Smoke, West Coast Magazine, Chapman.*
Earlier versions of some poems also appeared in the booklet *Spell
Bound,* Itinerant Publications, 1989.

Cover design: Fred Crayk

Printed by
Econoprint
55 Salamander Street
Leith

Contents

The Hill

The Morgan Boy

he ran
towards me
  bottle suspended
by teet
and teeth
  his body
covered
  slightly
by a grey vest
a collie
  at his side
at his other
an older brother
who asked

  if

I was a
proddy dog

  no

I'm a wee Scots girl

they aped
my lisp
in an Irish accent

Soda Bread

smells
hung
on the range
      we sat
in winceyette pyjamas
      not wanting
      to leave
the story filled room
the men
talked
as they drank
their medicine
the women
yawned
as they sipped their tea
remembering

to scold
us
off
to bed

The Byre

smells of
shit and warmth
clouded
four milkers
who stood
chained
to the stone wall
waiting
on release

a queue
of cats
crouched
waiting
for a line of milk
and

I knew
something

important
was about to happen
through
my Grand Father's
hands

Sunny Days

on sunny days
we would
    catch a cat
    tie it down
and if
it was
    secure
    enough

    we would
    fasten
a doll's bonnet
to its head
trundle the metal wheels
over the cobbles
saying
    "now now,
    good girls
    don't cry."

Curses

rose up
from beneath
our bed room
window
    we creaked
    over the boards
    on tip toe
    from
our iron ended bed

    shivered
    in the darkness

as Grampa
and Uncle Sam
sickled and scythed
in the moon light

Sometimes

during the day
I could hear
  the mice
  scurrying
  in the cupboard

where
  my pyjamas
were keeping warm
till night fall

Buried Treasure

Granny's room reeked
ancient riches
mother of pearl
glistened
on ebony black
ruby glass
hung
in long tinkles
brown twists
of dark wood
framed
the seat
    I lifted up
on the day
    when alone
    I found
    a pot
    of
shit

The Dark

the dark
wasn't the problem

it was when
he shone the torch
on my knickerless thighs
       I wanted to cry

as my brother
collected sixpences
from his mates
       and I
       got
       nothing

Bored Afternoons

on bored after noons
    I would sit
up the garden
    my head
    on my
    Grand Mother's
knee
that click clicked
arthritic knitting
half aware
of my return
to Scotland

totally in tune
    with the smells
    around me
    and Granny
    would say
MOVE

    or I'll knit
    your hair
    into a
dishcloth

Honour Bright

it took a silver bullet
to maim
my Grand Mother's witch
cousin
who turned into
a rabbit
or hare
as the mood
took

swam
up and down
Lough Neagh
fish-like
golden ear loops
in her gills

Grand Father willed
it was the truth

spat swore on his hand

"honour bright"
he would say
"honour bright"
in a way
that made
    my skin turn cold

and on the days
she'd come
for tea
from a dark and
hidden place
    I'd watch her limp
    in to my Granny's
    arms
    and
    walk with her
    down
    into the parlour
to talk of things

    we weren't
    allowed
    to hear

After Sunday School

in our best
frocks
and socks
we would
slink out
from kissing visitors
skip down
the twisting lane
to sit on the dyke
lady like
and wave
to passing motorists

but
if they didn't
wave back at us
we whispered
"bugger"

and laughed
out loud
all the way
home

Slopping Out

on the morning
of the day
they buried
my Grand Mother
my Aunt went
about
her usual chores
emptied pos
from under the beds
into
an old chipped bucket
topped it up
from the commode
then
carried it up
the garden
dug a hole
slopped it in
covered it over
then
dressed in black
sat at the back
of the car
that drove
them off
to the grave yard

A Know How Tae Suck Eggs

dae ye know whit he telt me
he said a looked like the Madonna
heh, mair like Bella Donna
an he said a walked like an angel
well it wis hard no tae believe
an then a remembered the six Bacardis
that a hud in the pub
an he telt me that he really went
fur intelligent girls
while he tried tae undo the top button
o ma new frock
that a hud picked an ironed special
well a telt him tae take a hike
a know a canny shuv ma granny aff a bus
know how?

she's deid.

Decay

the new moist cavity
of sponge gum
protected
from cold air
by hankie and scarf
is throbbing
to the beat
of my footsteps
and heart
as the paper seller
cries
of last night's rape
too late
to aid its victim
but in time
to sell news
two people and a pram
obstruct
the pavement
linked
with interest
in a mutual friend's
steamy affair
the child sleeps
and taxi horns
beep
warnings
to others
of traffic wardens
zoning in
on careless cars
and my mouth
fills
with more
than I can

swallow

Sour Note

and
as he took me
on the usual
week-end
spin
round his little
            finger
I tried hard
to ignore
his rose coloured passes
and said
            it was fun
while I lasted
but my heart
couldn't take
            much more

then
his eyes turned me
out of sight
and out of mine
came the pools
            I left
slowly seeping
into his floor

As Usual

claps and slaps
hyphenated
with curses
armour plated
lands her on the floor
where she can fall
no lower
than this
he has encouraged her
to stoop to

another night
another fight
him with his failure
her with his hobby
the voice of his authority
has woken the child
who screams
in harmony
with
her mother

and when he's done
having
nocturnal fun
she dries her disgrace
wipes the blood
from her face
and hums her baby
back
to the safety of sleep

as usual

Weekend Breaks

Saturday night
and seven o' clock
the children are in bed
dishes
in the sink
he is in the bathroom
and
she is on the brink
of
making up her mind
what to view
on the TV set

he is going through
after shaves
wondering which
will do the trick
counts his cash
swivels his hips
into his
week end strides

she counts stitches
on her pins
tucks her feet
up
in her chair
settles down
to get in to
an old romantic drama

*

8 o' clock
and in amongst
pals and pints
he is in the mood
for
talking big
laughing loud
telling girls
of how
he is
the answer to their

prayers
and if
they play
their cards
just right
he'll let them
touch
his belly flab
let them
kiss
him good night
let them
walk him
home

*

2 am
and in the living room
he is
shouting out
his usual
week end spiel
CALL YERSEL A FUCKIN WUMMIN
NAE WUNNER
A GET FUCKIN STEAMIN
COMIN HAME
TAE
FUCKIN THAT
AN LOOK AT ME
WHEN A TALK TAE YOU
A'LL TELL YOU
WHEN A'M
FUCKIN THROUGH

there are no
commercial breaks
in here
no kissing
make ups
no shining knight
on one
to pay
any heed
to her plight

and if
she screams
or
makes a sound
his fist will
make her
quieten down
turn her voice
into a whimper
make her
frightened
to wake
the neighbours

*

then,
at last,
his final thrust
he rolls
her over
straightens up
her recoiled limbs
and pumps
his prick
hard
into
her anus
bites her neck
until he comes
then
staggers off
to bed

*

Sunday morning
and the kids
shout about
whose turn it is
to be the banker
in the game
they've strewn across the floor

he is sitting
on the couch
checking out
his football coupon
shouting how
he could have won
had some one
scored a goal
and that
the referee
didn't
have a clue
and
if he saw him
in the street
he'd tell him
what
he could do

she is in the kitchenette
struggles to fry bacon
tries
hard
to hum along
to the singing
serviced hymns
that pour out loudly
from
the unviewed
television set

Memories Are Made of This

counting days backwards
to then
when we were
together
me in the prison
of your late night bars
you in your thirties
good job
and wife
to boot
yes
those were the days
of wine
and rows
of cracked ribs
with matching
cracking mind
matching
all our yesterdays
of lies
lacking
conviction
I still recall
like some masochist
the times we had together
just?
as if it were
yesterday
I cringe
in fear
of surprise attacking
and you
still as free
as the bird
that you will
never do

Night Life

ma maw goes oot
at night
ma faither does the same
an a stay at hame
an watch oor Jimmy
an wee Katy
she's the wean
a dinny mind it
aw the time
in fact sometimes
it's a laugh
like when we dress up
an carry oan
God
ye'd think we wur daft
or when we watch the folk
ower the road
comin oot the pub
they're iways shoutin
ur fightin an then
they go intae the chippy
fur some grub
but they iways end up
singin an staggerin
aw ower the place
wae their poke o chips
in their haun
tryin tae stuff
them in their face

sometimes
we're awfy fed up though
an we just sit
an don't talk
an we canny go oot
tae play
cause ma maw
pits oan the lock

anywi we're usually sleepin
when ma maw comes back hame
an then we wake up
CHRIST

it's iways the same
ma faither starts ragin
aboot wan thing ur another
then he slags ma maw's family
know
her sisters
an her brother
he disnae like them
much
though they seem aw right
tae me
but ma faither says
they're full o summit
cawed hypocricy

then he belts ma maw
an she starts tae scream

well maybe you think a'm silly
bit it's then
a start tae dream
aboot a warm bungalow
an ave a room o ma ane
an ma faither's iways singin
an ma maw
plays wae the wean

noo
a'm no complainin like
an a love ma maw
an ma faither
an a know
a'm dead lucky
cause they've really
stuck
the gither

but a wish it wis iways
day time
an everythin wis
cheery an bright

am eleven noo
bit a must be a big wean

cause secretly
a'm still feart
o the night

The Ignorant Bastard

she talks aboot
the ignorant bastard
she hopes
he's never set free
she caws him an ignorant bastard
fur whit he did
tae her
an me
a don't mind much aboot it
the times
she caws livin hell
but he must o bin
pretty awful
cos he's locked up
awe by hissel
a don't know
when he gets oot
an a really don't care
either
he can go
an rot in hell
that ignorant bastard
ma faither

Family Entertainment

when comfort
    left home
a scream
    rang out
windows
close their
    eyes
walls turned
    deaf ears

and
while someone
in the darkness
seed sowed
    against
nature
    dawn cracked
a girl child
    broke
and life
was never
the same

A Bag of Sweets

inside her mind
she lists places
counts faces
tries to think
where her son
might be

outside police men
in a field
in white shirt sleeves
on hands and knees
search
through blades of grass
for   tissues of evidence
           slices of cloth
           a small shoe
or sock

in the after noon heat
police start to treat
a dropped sweet
with care
samples of
           hair
           vomit
           and
           semen
are sent to a lab

police are sent to her door
we'd like to ask you
 once more
about the
           colour of his hair
           type of under wear
           do you recognise
this badge

her son's voice screams
in her head
still alive
never dead
she hears him call to her

           MUMMY!

Grandpa's Girl

she kisses her mother
good night
on the lips
and as she slips
her tongue
inside
her mouth
her hand
moves up
her thighs

her mother
tries
to disguise
disgust
and starts to focus
all her child's attention
on a book
of postman Pat
a black and white cat
or anything
but that
shadow
that points to their past

a past of pain
when she
went back
to work
again
unaware
that the man
she called dad
had had
her daughter
often
through the day
and now
therapist say
that if treated
with care
her nightmare
of incest

will slip inside
the recess
of her mind
and
when she comes
to marrying
the remaining
mental scarring
should be

Once

I slit
my tongue
for you
cut

it into
halves
and
quarters
so
only
the smallest
of peeps
could
emit
still

your ears
never heard
never
     once
         heard
my adoration
of you

Daddy

I was a stranger
in your eyes
I unnerved
the you
     that talked
     graciously
     to those
     you wished
to indent
socially
     we missed

days
at the zoo
at the park
or even....

my list runs short
for that is
all I wanted
once

I wore
a pretty dress
ribbons
in my hair
        they were blue
and you
took me
by the wrist
all the way

to market
to show me
the happy Christmas turkey
being strangled

Sweet Seventeen

the public convenience
of an oblivious
industrial town
on a raining Wednesday after noon
hides
the flesh filled super market bag
that is tidily tied
at the top
to stop
the tiniest breath of life

and the girl of seventeen

whose future was forced
by four fourteen-year-old
glue-sniffing lads
that laughed
as they had
her time and again
in the rain
as she struggled
home alone
from a friend
who
told her to
take care

is sorting things out

as dry-eyed
she cuts her losses
and
slits her wrists

The Day the Rot Set in

clear water once flowed
under these bridges
that now stagnate
with human remains
of twelve year old mothers
feeding the pimps
who fix their lives
nicely
through
the bend of their arms
as the kind man hotly
takes their picture
while God
pushing heaven
for a penny's worth of faith
is immune to the smell
of sympathy
that scuffles and troubles
the eyes
of the men
who question the path
they already walk

(and i think)
(when i remember to)

of these streets
of litter
these pavements of
cracks
and crap
and crack
that drags the sight seers
through gutterish dead oceans
of youth
going
nowhere
drifting
through national front ranks
bursting
their special smiles
into clouds of
hate
as the holocaust spreads
and we
sleep on

An Act of Love

She
is sitting
poised,
confident.
Life's beating blows
shows
no signs
on this
thickly made up
sickly fed up
face.

Her husband
is by her side
fulfilling her
every command.

She works him
like an organ grinder
with a performing
monkey
and laughs
at how easy
it is
to turn his love
for her
into a stage
for an undercover
thespian.

Left Overs

sausages spitting in the frying pan
sun shine segments lighting the wall
children clattering on the stairs

it's Saturday morning and your smile
didn't break your fall this time
only your back and your neck

and I'm not there
as they talk your life
in the co-op funeral parlour,
or standing around
as you enter the ground
in front of your wife
who thought I was nice
but didn't know me
so well

and anyway
what's the difference

you've gone
and the bacon
is burning

Reflections

when young
at school
learning
my lessening lessons
the ones that taught me
to say grace
and
know my place
or tried
but lied
to me
about Uncle God
was when I found out
what things
were about
like flowers in my hair
and all the Woodstock wear
and that
boys never tired
of their constant desire
to get my knickers
off

I kept mine on
for their interest
would stay
a little longer
that way
and

then
in the middle of
chewing gum
and cries of
show us yer
chibs
tongs ya bass
and bundy boys live
one night
at a
hash-in
which was then
quite

the fashion
I smoked my first joint
and thought
      what's the whole point
      of being familiar
      with psychedelia
so I pleased Dad and Mum
and grew up some
and then some more
      OH GOD
      WHAT
      A
      BORE

Mrs him and two point four sibs
he still carried his chib
and a mortgage as well
I screamed
"Bloody Hell"
and went back
to a happier
day

which
by the way
when I turned
my new leaf
I had fewer
real teeth
and I now share my dentures
with pre-senile dementia
the occasional bile
arthritis
and piles
but I'm not complaining
as my eyesight starts failing
for never the less
I am now
at my best

Cycling

and
as the time drew near
I waited
to see
a sign
to relieve apprehension
as sometimes
you do
when something
is due
a little too delicate
to mention

so without more ado
I went to the loo
deciding
to scrutinise
the area
for some signs of menstruation
cervical dilation
or even
bloody malaria
which ever
those firsts
couldn't be worse
than a late
impregnation

on hoping to find
a positive sign
I commenced the search at once
but what was there
made me despair
so much
I forgot
about lunch

there was a spoon
from the set
that I happened to get
at Aunt Mary's silver wedding
and a picture card

from someone in Largs
I couldn't tell

for the writing was fading
there was a cup
a plate
a prune
and a date
and a Beezer nineteen eighty two annual
a bicycle pump
grapes in a clump
and a Citroën handbook manual
as I dug in deeper
I found a sweater
and a jigsaw puzzle piece
I thought
this was fun
    as I pulled out a gun
and a set
of plastic
    false teeth

I thought
it's about time
this orifice of mine
was cleaned out
once and for all
and my eyes opened wide
as things lay
side by side
for they stretched up
the length of the hall
I was in a state
as I looked at the date
on my calendar
of Diana and Chairlie

then I sighed with relief
as I pulled down
    my sleeve
for you see
    I was one week
too early

Left on the Shelf

double barrelled legs
carries old Meg
past flannelette shelves

she is eighty nine
and wants something
fine
and feminine

sifting through
basques
of satin and silk
and cloth
of that ilk
she searches to find
a particular kind
for her larger than life
soaked body

her chin is stubbled
with hairs
and the coat that she wears
is wind strong and woolly
to match the hat
that keeps her warm
personality
cozy

something pink
or black
she mutters back
to the girl
who tries to help
the watery eyes
that can't find
the size

it would be nice
she says
to get
a front
fastening set
that dries quickly
when wet

instead of a simmit

does underwear
have a limit?

Allowances

odours ooze
from her bulging body
police messages
crackle
from her
bulging bag
onlisteners
strain
with curiosity
wishing to know
the why and the what
of what she's got
in the out of date
out of order
Union Jack shopper
but not the what
and the why
of the smell
that goes by
streaming
nose
and eye

still

she stands
in the Post Office queue
waiting her turn
to cash her cheque
to pay her way
while
spraying smiles
of sunshine showers
at the few
who dare
look into
her eyes

This Town is Full

of
everything you want
and a little bit more
from the Presto store
that pushy pensioners
think
they have the right to

full of
winter breaks
slipping of snow
cracking your ankle
because
the Council
won't
fix the pavements
full of
the privileged few
who can
afford
the school dinner queue

this town is full
of whelks from Saltcoats
glowing
in the dark
of packs of dogs
roaming like casuals
through the schemes
full of young boys
getting beaten
because police
like
to enforce
law and order

this town is full
of gents toilets
full
of trawling hopefuls
ladies toilets
always closed

this town is full
of purple nosed
winos
in the park
sharing a can
before
it gets dark
full of
expensive flats
common as muck
of
battered wives
scared to leave home
in the middle
of the night
in case
they get mugged
of packs of casuals
roaming like dogs
through the schemes

full of librium
      valium
      some
      temgesics,
      oh
      and
      a
      pan
      loaf
      please

of grave yards
full
of forgotten folk
buried beneath
empty crisp pokes
      carlsberg cans
            nail vanish bottles
this town
is full
of shite

48

this town is full
of doffers
spinners
folk that made school dinners
used to be
steel pressers
work assessors
lots of wee hairdressers
ex
ship builders
spot welders
lots of bewildered school leavers
all wondering

when the shops'll shut

Hospital Efficiency and the Smell of Success

incontinency
punctuates
the nurses' day
with a supported
after meal
slipper shuffle to toilets
and back to chairs
where they'll remain
till fed again
these acutely insane
women

the ward sister
who stays at her station
has decided on
a regulation
of the bowels

liquid paraffin's
the medication
freely given
to every patient
for constipation

the increased frequency
of defecation
will also keep
the nurses
on their toes

a quiet calm
of an afternoon
has broken into
an all too soon
cacophony of moans
groans
fits

and farts
as the major
clean up starts

hospital issued
crimplene dresses
are hurriedly discarded

into heaped up messes
of plastic laundry bags
and active patients
speed in
out
through toilet doors
as nurses try
to clear the floors
in case of
further accidents

and faeces
freely smushed
into fingers
faces
down the front
of new donned dresses
and through the hair
of motionless
middle aged
motherless masses
curled in chairs
unaware
of anything
in
or out

and
whilst others
hysterically create
about the stench
the appalling rate
human waste
sludges round the ward

in the office
sister sits
cleanly white
no signs of shit
she gives an almost humorous chort
while filling in the ward report
having shut the door
against the smell
she writes

all patients' bowels
are working well

Joan

steam trickles
down the asylum's
ancient
windows and
walls
that stop watchers peering in
patients from fleeing out
and
inside the weekly wash room
females paddle
semi clad in
and out
of showers

the door
is locked
with a big key
that stays shut
inside
the nurse's pocket
she mixes orders
and bath water
nakeds
all the women
with a practised
flick
of the wrist

seven women
in the room
drip
exposing every crevice
except for one

the one in charge
turns the hot tap off
tests the water
takes Joan
by the skin
"get in"

Joan sees
neither
bath
shower
or our
understanding of life
only
her
coffin
tempts
and teases
yawning wide
waiting
for her
to step
inside
be incased
alive
for ever
and bare flesh
slaps
on sodden floors

the nurse
stands at the wooden doors
takes a sneaky soggy puff

sister drags on her mind
wages clink in her head

"get in"

she says

Joan screams
in her face
patients scream
in between
showers
orderlies
come to the rescue

later

seven nurses
in the wash
room
all dressed

the same
except
for Joan
in the bath
    whose screams
clamber on the asylum's walls
    that bar watchers
from peering in
patients from fleeing out

Bella

look at the size o that
Bella said
as she cradled
a hot steaming shite
from the unlocked toilets
as if it was
a fragile fortune
as if it was
some unwanted orphan
as if it was her long awaited child

she strutted through the ward

thirty years before
her husband
strutted through the war

and

glory filled
Bella had danced
her man
came back
from the war
with stockings, stories
and a long line of gory tales
of dying men
and wandering WAFFs
but never mentioned
the campaigns
of
his untouchable barge pole
that put Bella
in an asylum
for the rest
of her life

gonorrhoea
syphilis
medals from the king

Bella carried the shite
tenderly

the ward sister
told her
to put it back where she got it

largactal burned in her mind
tears burned in her eyes

but obediently
Bella stuffed her thoughts
and dreams
down the drain
of the hospital sink

Mary

is
in the geriatric chair
wrapped tightly
in a blanket
that has white squares

she does not see
the strutting woman
the tendered domestic
or the hypodermics
that prick her
three times a day

her pupils transfix
exposed
onto
nothingness

she is
outwardly dead
mechanically sound

sister smiles on her rounds
everything is neat and tidy

Mary lies
eyes
open

eight hour shifts change

Mary lies
eyes
open

"she is catatonic
lost
for days
and days"
someone
experienced says

and
nurses fill
in time
by tucking the blanket
smoothing her hair

shifting the chair
from here
        to there
allowing domestics
to clean
the carpet
wipe up
the menstrual blood
that drips
        now
and then

Linda

Linda is in the dining room
she is thirty two
and has a hard plastic bib
round her neck

around her mouth
she has bits
of the butchered meat
she refused to eat
at lunch time

Linda is vegetarian

from her hair drops
the mince
she threw at the nurse
who crunched the spoon
against her teeth
squeezed her nose
till she
couldn't breath
packed her mouth
when she
gasped for air
held
it shut
rubbed her throat
made her choke

it was then she threw the mince

Linda is in the geriatric chair
staff nurse said
leave her there
till
tea time

The Man with the Badges

it is
three o' clock
in the after noon
and in the hospital grounds
he wears pyjamas
and over
coat

a cord drips
below its hem
sways
in rhythm
to his foot
to foot
to
foot
stamp

his saliva grin
gushes wide
when he blocks
plumbers
porters
window cleaners
in their stride

ANY BADGES?

his hands shake
in the wake
of
largactil
penbritin
epanuton
paraldehide

his coat is plastered
with mucus
rain
and badges
with

doctor names
nurses names
happy smiles
Glasgow's miles
better
tufty club
Beelzebub
Morecambe
Woolacombe
ban the bomb
and one
that some
one gave him once
don't laugh at me
I'm nuts

ANY BADGES
ANY BADGES
ANY BADGES

is all he ever says
every day
to every one
who passes through
the hospital gates

as he stands
hands

out stretched
unaware of the wind
fanning his hair
flooding
his coat
shivering through
his sodden
slippers

Visiting

Hi Mum
I'm back
yes
too long
but now
I'm here
with flowers
no tears
so long
water   bridges
you know
still
still
a lot
between us
six feet
of earth
holding you
down

Ma Mither

ma mither's deid ye know
she buckled ma heid ye know

so did her death

It's Only a Nightmare

I lie
and listen
to silence

not the clock
or the wind
or the ringing
in my ear
or the heart beat
in my head

but silence

as I start nocturnal fixing
to stay away
from the screams
in the night
in my head
fighting
silence
with silence
reflecting

reflections
of kidding my self
with drink
and pills
and pop
another victim
on the video
of life
for the living
and dying
and dreaming
of other than this
garbage heaped horror world
called home
from the war

fought
to another
that's not
but could be
if dreams were freed
nightmares caught
and
silence sound

Biographical Note

Margaret Fulton Cook was born and still lives in Paisley. Her work has been published in various magazines throughout the British Isles, in France, America and has been translated into Spanish. A collection of her poetry *Spell Bound* was published in 1989. She is well known as a live performer and has appeared in many venues throughout Scotland, England and including Barlinnie prison. As well as speaking at writing seminars she has also set up and tutored a number of writers workshops in and around Glasgow. She has edited anthologies of short stories and poetry and produced a number of plays which have been performed in Glasgow. She is a former managing editor of West Coast magazine. She is working on her next collection and says that her driving force is to give voice to those who scream in silence.